HISTORIC PLACES *of the* UNITED KINGDOM

ANGLO-SAXON SITES

Nancy Dick

raintree

Raintree is an imprint of Capstone Global Library Limited, a company incorporated in England and Wales having its registered office at 264 Banbury Road, Oxford, OX2 7DY – Registered company number: 6695582

www.raintree.co.uk

myorders@raintree.co.uk

Produced for Raintree by

White-Thomson Publishing Ltd

+44 (0)1273 477 216

www.wtpub.co.uk

Edited by Nancy Dickmann
Designed by Clare Nicholas
Original illustrations © Capstone Global Library Ltd 2017
Illustrated by Ron Dixon
Production by Duncan Gilbert
Originated by Capstone Global Library Ltd
Printed and bound in India

ISBN 978 1 4747 5409 5 (hardcover)
21 20 19 18 17
10 9 8 7 6 5 4 3 2 1

ISBN 978 1 4747 5420 0 (paperback)
22 21 20 19 18
10 9 8 7 6 5 4 3 2 1

British Library Cataloguing in Publication Data
A full catalogue record for this book is available from the British Library.

Acknowledgements
We would like to thank the following for permission to reproduce photographs: Adam Stanford © Aerial-Cam Ltd, 18 (right), 24; Alamy: Ashley Cooper, 15, Eyre, 22, Graeme Peacock, 14, Gretchen Mattison, 7, Joana Kruse, cover, 17, Loop Images Ltd, 12, 18 (left), Purple Marbles York, 4, Quantum Images, 8, The Photolibrary Wales, 6; istockphoto: JacquiMD, 28, whitemay, 20–21; Shutterstock: chrisdorney, 13, 29, Daniel Buxton Photography, 3, 11, 23, 31, Diana Mower, 1, 10, Flik47, 21, Matthew J Thomas, 16, Peter Lorimer, 9, 19, 25, RG-vc, 27, Victor Maschek, 26.

We would like to thank Philip Parker for his help in the preparation for this book.

CONTENTS

Some words are shown in bold, **like this**. You can find out what they mean by looking in the glossary.

WHO WERE THE ANGLO-SAXONS?

Two thousand years ago, Britain was ruled by the Romans. The **native** Britons had got used to having the Roman army to protect them. But in AD 410, the last Roman officials left Britain. This left Britain open to invasion. It was soon overrun by people that we now call the Anglo-Saxons.

Invaders

In the AD 400s, people from Ireland attacked England from the west. People from Scotland attacked from the north. Boats from the lands that are now Germany and Denmark landed along the east coast. They carried Anglo-Saxon **raiders** and **settlers**. The Anglo-Saxons settled the eastern areas, then moved westwards. By the AD 600s, they were the dominant group on the island.

Even today, re-enactors bring Anglo-Saxon history to life.

Lasting legacy

Many of the Anglo-Saxons settled down permanently in their new home. They set up several different kingdoms and made laws. They brought their art, culture and stories. They fought to protect their new home from **Viking** invaders. Their language and legends are part of British culture today. They left behind buildings and **artefacts** that can still be seen.

This map shows the most important Anglo-Saxon kingdoms by AD 600.

DIG DEEPER

** ANGLES, SAXONS AND JUTES **

The people that we now call Anglo-Saxons were originally separate groups: the Angles, Saxons and Jutes. (Most of the native Britons called them all Saxons.) By the 8th century, they had begun to call themselves Angli or English.

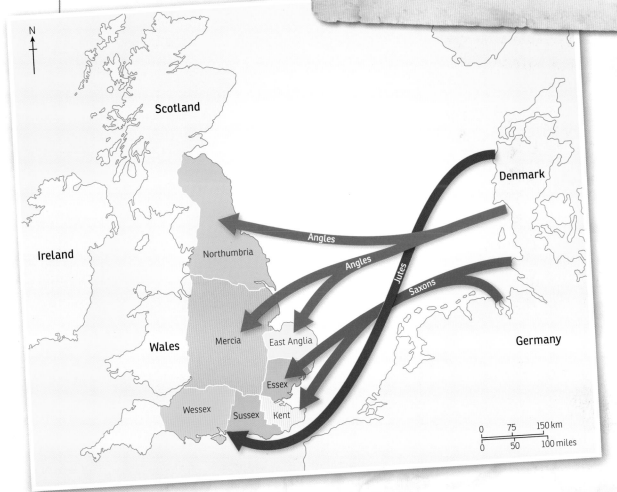

OFFA'S DYKE

A massive earthen wall still snakes through Wales and western England. It was built to form an imposing barrier between two kingdoms. It is known as Offa's **Dyke** and is named after the Anglo-Saxon king who is thought to have ordered its construction.

OFFA'S DYKE

Warring kingdoms

The Anglo-Saxons who settled in Britain did not form a united nation. Instead, they split up into smaller kingdoms. The most powerful kingdoms were Northumbria, Mercia, East Anglia, Wessex and Kent. There were smaller kingdoms too. These kingdoms sometimes cooperated but sometimes fought against each other. They also fought against the other groups living in Britain.

WHAT: defensive earthwork

WHERE: near the Wales–England border

WHEN: probably between AD 757 and AD 796

A deep ditch next to a high wall would have made it difficult for armies to cross Offa's Dyke.

Dyke details

Offa's Dyke formed a long barrier between the Anglo-Saxon kingdom of Mercia and the Welsh kingdom of Powys. About 129 kilometres (80 miles) can still be seen, but it was originally longer. It is a high earthen wall that may have had wood or stone structures at the top. On the Welsh side, there is a deep ditch.

DIG DEEPER

** WHO WAS OFFA? **

Offa became king of Mercia in AD 757. He ruled until his death in AD 796. Offa was a strong ruler who conquered several smaller kingdoms. He also formed strong relationships with other European rulers.

Offa led the Mercian army in many battles.

How was the dyke built?

Workers probably dug the ditch first and then used the leftover soil to build the mound next to it. It would have taken a large workforce a long time to build the dyke. The workers only had simple hand tools, such as wooden spades. In Anglo-Saxon times, ordinary people had to spend a certain amount of time working for their ruler. This is probably how Offa found enough men to do the digging and mound building.

DIG DEEPER

** FLEAM DYKE **

Fleam Dyke is another example of an Anglo-Saxon dyke. It runs for about 5 kilometres (3 miles) through Cambridgeshire, although it may have once been longer. It may have been built by the East Anglians for protection against Mercian invaders.

Fleam Dyke has been turned into a beautiful walking path.

Other dykes

Offa's Dyke was not the first of its kind. In fact, **archaeologists** have recently shown that parts of the wall may have been built hundreds of years before Offa's time. There are similar dykes in many other parts of Britain. Some were built by the Anglo-Saxons, and others were built by the Britons.

Later defences

Starting in AD 793, **Viking raiders** began to target Britain. Dykes were not enough to keep them out. Under Alfred the Great (AD 849–899), the Anglo-Saxons started to build fortified towns called *burhs*. Some made use of old Roman walls, while others were built from scratch. The burhs were connected by roads.

The Anglo-Saxons used spears and axes, like the ones shown here, to fight off invaders. They also used swords and bows and arrows.

CHAPEL OF SAINT PETER-ON-THE-WALL

One of England's oldest buildings stands near the windy Essex coast. The tiny **chapel** of St Peter-on-the-Wall marks a turning point in British history: the time when its residents began to **convert** to Christianity.

ST PETER-ON-THE-WALL

Pagan beginnings

There had been some Christians in Britain since Roman times. But when the Anglo-Saxons came, they brought their own religion. They believed in many of the same gods as the **Vikings**. They also believed that lucky charms could protect them from danger and disease.

WHAT: Christian church

WHERE: near Bradwell-on-Sea, Essex

WHEN: AD 654

Today, the tiny church is surrounded by farmland. It is still used for religious services.

Building the chapel

In AD 597, the Pope sent a **monk** called Augustine to convert the people of Britain to Christianity. Christianity also spread back into Britain from Ireland. In the AD 650s, a monk called Cedd, who was trained in the Irish tradition, travelled south from Northumbria to spread the Christian word. The chapel was built as a place for his new converts to gather.

Anglo-Saxon **artefacts** show their Christian faith. This strip of gold, found in 2009, has a quote from the Bible on it.

DIG DEEPER

** DAYS OF THE WEEK **

Some of the days of the week are named after Anglo-Saxon gods. Tuesday comes from Tiw, the god of war. Wednesday means "Woden's day", after Woden, the king of the gods. Thursday comes from Thunor, god of thunder, and Friday is from Frige, goddess of love.

Two branches

There were two main forms of Christianity in Anglo-Saxon times. Monks from Ireland taught the Celtic form of Christianity, mainly in the north. Augustine's form of Christianity was more closely linked to Rome. Both groups built monasteries, where monks prayed, worked and copied out books. The monasteries were the only schools in Britain.

The rise of Christianity

By the time of Alfred the Great, who ruled from AD 871–899, most Anglo-Saxons had converted. Alfred was a **devout** Christian who thought that raids by **pagan** Vikings were punishment from God. He saw his stunning victory over the Vikings at the battle of Ethandun as a victory for Christianity. People's faith in Christianity increased, and more chapels were built.

Monks lived a simple life. The inside of St Peter-on-the-Wall is simple too, with little decoration.

DIG DEEPER

** RECYCLING MATERIALS **

After the Romans left Britain, many of their buildings were abandoned. There was a Roman fort near St Peter-on-the-Wall. Many of its stones were reused to build the chapel. This type of recycling was very common in Anglo-Saxon times.

Anglo-Saxon churches

A few Anglo-Saxon churches still survive, and many more have Anglo-Saxon parts. Most would have been built from wood and **thatch**. However, nearly all the churches that have survived are stone or brick. Stones in a **herringbone** pattern and windows with triangular tops are typical Anglo-Saxon features.

Holy Trinity Church in Colchester, Essex, has a beautiful Saxon tower. It was built from reused Roman bricks.

BEWCASTLE CROSS

The remains of Bewcastle Cross tower over the headstones in the churchyard of St Cuthbert's. Even though its crosspiece and top are missing, this stone cross stands about 4.5 metres (15 feet) high. Its beautiful carvings make it a powerful symbol of Christianity in Anglo-Saxon times.

BEWCASTLE STONE CROSS

WHAT: stone cross

WHERE: Bewcastle, Cumbria

WHEN: probably between AD 670 and 750

The top part, or crosspiece, has been lost over time. Now only the **shaft** remains.

shaft

Stone crosses

Stone crosses were common in Anglo-Saxon Britain. Some of them marked places where people could gather to listen to **sermons**. Some were put up in sites that **pagans** believed were holy. Others were erected near Christian churches. Many of the stone crosses from this period had a circle surrounding the crosspiece and the shaft.

Carvings

There are carvings on each of the four sides of the Bewcastle cross. One side shows Jesus and John the Baptist. The other three sides have animals, vines, knots and even a sundial. There are also panels with writing in the **runic alphabet**. This early writing style was later replaced with the alphabet that we use today.

crosspiece

circle

DIG DEEPER

** MIXING PAGAN AND CHRISTIAN **

The stone cross at Gosforth was built a few hundred years after the one at Bewcastle. By then, **Vikings** had settled there. The carvings on this cross show Christian symbols as well as characters from Viking **mythology**. Some historians think this shows that Norse stories were used to illustrate Christian teachings.

Gosforth Cross, in Cumbria, still has its crosspiece and the circle around it.

WEST STOW

Anglo-Saxons built their homes from wood and **thatch**, which rotted away over time. There are none left standing today. **Archaeologists** have found the remains of an Anglo-Saxon village in Suffolk. They used what they learned to build **replicas**, or copies, of the type of house that the Anglo-Saxons lived in.

WEST STOW

Local materials

When the Romans left Britain around AD 410, they abandoned their buildings, which were built from brick or stone. The Anglo-Saxons tended not to use these towns. They preferred to clear forests to build new settlements. They chose locations near sources of food and water and built wooden homes. Villages were surrounded by a fence to keep out wild animals.

WHAT: Anglo-Saxon village

WHERE: West Stow, Suffolk

WHEN: probably between AD 420 and 650

In Anglo-Saxon times, much of England was covered in forests, providing plenty of wood for building.

Simple homes

Ordinary Anglo-Saxons lived in simple, one-room houses. An entire family would share this single room. They used it for cooking, sleeping and entertaining. Smoke from a central fire escaped through a hole in the roof. Houses had tiny windows with no glass. The houses were angled to catch as much sunlight as possible.

DIG DEEPER

** WATTLE AND DAUB **

Some Anglo-Saxon homes were built using wattle and daub. Wattle and daub used small wooden branches that were woven together to form a wall. The walls were then smeared with mud or clay, mixed with straw, horsehair and even animal dung. This mixture dried like plaster.

The reconstructed buildings at West Stow show how the Anglo-Saxons lived.

Halls

Each village would have a hall, where the chief and his family lived. These buildings were made of wood and thatch, similar to ordinary houses. But they were much larger – one found in Somerset was 18 metres (60 feet) long and 9 metres (30 feet) wide. A hall was big enough for some of the chief's men to live there too.

The furniture in a hall was simple and made of wood.

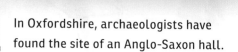

In Oxfordshire, archaeologists have found the site of an Anglo-Saxon hall.

Feasts and stories

Few Anglo-Saxons could read, so they often entertained each other by singing and telling stories. At night, villagers might gather round the fire in the chief's hall to eat and drink. Skilled storytellers would recount legends about adventures and heroes, such as Beowulf.

DIG DEEPER

** FOOD AND DIET **

Anglo-Saxons ate mainly bread, porridge and vegetables. They also ate fruit and eggs, and their cows and goats provided milk. Meat was a rare treat for ordinary people. They used honey to sweeten food and to make a drink called mead. Anglo-Saxons drank weak beer instead of water because the water in rivers was too dirty.

The Anglo-Saxon diet was based on the foods they could grow on their farms.

Family life

Most Anglo-Saxons were simple farmers, and the father was head of the family. Alongside his farm work, he had to be ready to defend the village from enemies. His wife was responsible for cooking, cleaning, weaving and looking after the children. Most children did not go to school. Instead, they helped their parents and learned from them.

SUTTON HOO

In 1939, an amazing burial site was found in Suffolk. Beneath a large mound, there had once been an entire Anglo-Saxon ship. Its wooden planks had rotted away, but it was packed with gold and silver treasures. There were more graves surrounding the mound.

SUTTON HOO

WHAT: ship burial

WHERE: near Woodbridge, Suffolk

WHEN: probably between AD 600 and 650

DIG DEEPER

** DISCOVERING SUTTON HOO **

People had known for hundreds of years that the mounds at Sutton Hoo were burial sites. Another mound on the site had been robbed by tomb raiders. In 1938, an **archaeologist** called Basil Brown (1888–1977) began to dig. He found the buried ship the following year.

More than a dozen burial mounds were found at Sutton Hoo.

Beautiful treasure

The ship contained a sword, shield and helmet, as well as a coat of **chain mail**. There were also dishes, cups, spoons and drinking horns. There were even beautiful items made of precious metals and gemstones. These treasures are now on display at the British Museum in London.

Who was it?

Nobody was found in the ship burial. However, chemicals in the soil show that there may have been a body, which decayed and disappeared. Because of the expensive items found in the ship, it must have been a very important person, maybe even a king. Some historians think it was Rædwald, who was king of East Anglia around the time the ship was buried.

A metal helmet was found in pieces. This **replica** shows what it would have looked like.

Anglo-Saxon kings

Each group of Anglo-Saxons had a leader who would lead them in battle. Anglo-Saxon men swore an oath of loyalty to their leader. Successful leaders became kings. A king upheld the law and customs. There were several different kingdoms, and they often fought each other. By conquering another kingdom, a king could get rich.

Defending the land

Once the **Vikings** invaded, the Anglo-Saxon kings did not work together well to fight back. As a result, their lands were all conquered except for Alfred the Great's kingdom of Wessex. Alfred and his children and grandchildren were eventually able to regain the rest of the land. It became part of a single united kingdom of England.

This is how archaeologists think the ship was arranged before it was buried.

Why a ship?

Burying the body at Sutton Hoo in a ship was a way of showing his status. Ships were incredibly important to the Anglo-Saxons. They were used for travel and trade. Travelling by ship was often quicker and easier than going by land. The ship at Sutton Hoo was 27 metres (89 feet) long. It may have had a mast for sailing the ocean or just oars for rowing along rivers and coasts.

DIG DEEPER

** METALWORK **

The Anglo-Saxons were known for their beautiful metalwork. They shaped gold into complicated patterns and often set it with pieces of **garnet**. Several pieces in this style were found at Sutton Hoo. They included clasps for holding pieces of **armour** together and the lid of a decorated purse.

This piece of an Anglo-Saxon sword handle is decorated with complicated knot patterns.

HEYSHAM ROCK-CUT TOMBS

On a windy cliff on the Lancashire coast, six holes have been cut into a block of solid rock. They are clearly graves of some sort, but they are empty. Nobody knows who was buried there, or why.

HEYSHAM

Cut into stone

Two of the six graves are rectangular, and the other four are shaped like human bodies. Five of them have another small hole at the head end. Historians think that these holes were for holding the **shaft** of a wooden cross.

WHAT: series of tombs

WHERE: Heysham, Lancashire

WHEN: probably between AD 900 and 1000

Anyone visiting the graves would see dramatic views out across Morecambe Bay.

Anglo-Saxon burial

It would have taken a lot of work to cut the graves. This makes it likely that important people were buried in them. Most Anglo-Saxons were buried or **cremated** after they died. Only rich, important people were buried in mounds or in rock-cut tombs. People were sometimes buried with jewellery, weapons and offerings of food and drink.

After a body was burned on a **pyre**, the remains were put in an urn like this and buried.

DIG DEEPER

** PILGRIM TRAIL **

The ruins of a small **chapel** stand near the tombs. The chapel was built in the AD 700s. It was dedicated to St Patrick, who is famous for bringing Christianity to Ireland. The chapel in Heysham was an important site for **pilgrims**. They would come there to pray.

YOUR LOCAL AREA

The Anglo-Saxons settled all over England. One of their most lasting legacies isn't a building, a grave or a **dyke**. Instead, it is their language. The English that we speak is based on the language that the Anglo-Saxons used. Their version lives on in many of our place names.

Invaders

Britain has been invaded many times, and each group tried to put their own stamp on their new home. Like other groups, the Anglo-Saxons used their own language to name the towns and cities they built. We still use many of these names today.

The east of England is full of Anglo-Saxon names such as Norwich, which means "north settlement".

Anglo-Saxon words

Anglo-Saxon place names are made up of smaller words. They describe a place's setting or its purpose. Here are just a few of them:

Word	Meaning	Example
burh	fortified town	Peterborough
burn	stream	Burnham
combe	small valley	Bincombe
ford	shallow river crossing	Oxford
ham	village	Birmingham
stow	meeting place or holy place	Walthamstow
wic	farm or settlement	Norwich

DIG DEEPER

** ACTIVITY **

If you live in England, take a look at a map of your local area. Can you find any villages, towns or cities that have Anglo-Saxon names? Do they match up with the natural features in their meanings, such as valleys or rivers? If you live in a different part of the country, try to spot the Anglo-Saxon names in other areas.

"Burh" can be written as "bury" or "borough". Canterbury means "Kentish fortified town".

TO Deal 6 Miles.

TO Canterbury 12 Miles. London 68 Miles.

THE END OF THE ANGLO-SAXONS

During the Anglo-Saxon period, different groups constantly struggled for power. In 1016, England was even conquered by a **Viking** king called Cnut. After the deaths of Cnut and his sons, Anglo-Saxons took over again. But Anglo-Saxon rule did not last for much longer.

Here come the Normans

In 1066, an Anglo-Saxon named Harold Godwinson was king of England. He was related to Cnut by marriage. When an army from Normandy landed on the south coast near Hastings, a great battle followed. The **Normans** won the battle, and Harold was killed. The Norman leader, William, became king. There would be no more Anglo-Saxon kings.

Alfred the Great once ruled from Winchester. The Normans replaced its Anglo-Saxon cathedral with a new cathedral.

Timeline

AD 410	The last Roman troops leave Britain.
around AD 420	An Anglo-Saxon village is built at West Stow.
AD 597	Augustine arrives in Britain to **convert** the people to Christianity.
AD 600–650	At some point during this time, an important leader is buried in a ship at Sutton Hoo.
AD 654	The **chapel** of St Peter-on-the-Wall is built.
AD 670–750	A large carved stone cross is erected in Bewcastle.
AD 757	Offa becomes king of Mercia.
	Offa's **Dyke** may have been built during his reign, which ended in AD 796.
AD 793	The first **Viking** raid in Britain takes place on the island of Lindisfarne.
AD 871	Alfred the Great becomes king of Wessex.
AD 899	Alfred the Great dies.
AD 900–1000	Six tombs are carved out of the rock in Heysham.
1016	Cnut of Denmark becomes king of England.
1066	The last Anglo-Saxon king, Harold Godwinson, is killed at the Battle of Hastings.
	William the Conqueror becomes king.
1939	The ship burial at Sutton Hoo is discovered.

Glossary

archaeologist person who learns about the past by digging up old buildings or objects and studying them

armour metal covering worn for protection during battle

artefact object used in the past that was made by people

chain mail armour made of thousands of tiny iron rings linked together

chapel small church or a section in a larger church

convert change from one religion to another, or persuade someone else to change religion

cremate burn a dead body to ashes

devout deeply religious

dyke large wall made of earth that is used as a barrier

garnet hard, dark-red mineral that is often used in jewellery

herringbone pattern of rows of parallel lines with every second row slanting in the opposite direction

monk man who lives in a religious community and promises to devote his life to his religion

mythology old stories told again and again that connect people with their past

native originally living in a certain place

Norman member of a group of people with Scandinavian ancestry who moved to northern France in the AD 900s

pagan person who worships many gods instead of just one

pilgrim person who travels to a holy place for religious reasons

pyre pile of wood built to burn a dead body for a funeral

raider person who launches a sudden, surprise attack on a place

replica exact copy of something

runic alphabet old system of writing used by the Anglo-Saxons and Vikings

sermon religious talk

settler person who makes a home in a new place

shaft long, straight part of a cross, which supports the crosspiece

thatch covering for houses made of straw or grass

Vikings Scandinavian warriors who invaded Europe and North America between the 8th and 11th centuries

Find out more

BOOKS

Anglo-Saxons (Fact Cat History: Early Britons), Izzi Howell (Wayland, 2016)

Anglo-Saxons (Writing History), Anita Ganeri (Franklin Watts, 2017)

The Battle of Hastings (Why Do We Remember?), Claudia Martin (Franklin Watts, 2016)

Life in Anglo-Saxon Britain (A Child's History of Britain), Anita Ganeri (Raintree, 2015)

WEBSITES

www.bbc.co.uk/education/topics/zxsbcdm
Go here to find learning guides about the Anglo-Saxons.

www.bbc.co.uk/history/ancient/anglo_saxons/overview_anglo_saxons_01.shtml
Here you'll find a more detailed history of the Anglo-Saxon period.

www.dkfindout.com/uk/history/anglo-saxons/
This site is chock-full of facts about the Anglo-Saxons.

www.natgeokids.com/uk/discover/history/general-history/anglo-saxons/
Want to learn some awesome Anglo-Saxon facts? Try this website.

PLACES TO VISIT

Birmingham Museum and Art Gallery
(home of the Stafforshire Hoard, the largest hoard of Anglo-Saxon gold ever found)
Birmingham, B3 3DH

The British Museum
(home of many Anglo-Saxon treasures)
London, WC1B 3DG

Jarrow Hall
(Anglo-Saxon Farm and Village)
Jarrow, South Tyneside, NE32 3DY

Offa's Dyke Centre
(Anglo-Saxon earthwork)
Knighton, Powys, LD7 1EN

St Cuthbert's Church
(site of the Bewcastle Cross)
Bewcastle, Cumbria, CA6 6PS

St Peter-on-the-Wall
(Anglo-Saxon chapel)
Bradwell-on-Sea, Essex, CM0 7PN

St Peter's Church
(site of rock-cut tombs)
Heysham, Lancashire, LA3 2RN

Sutton Hoo
(site of Anglo-Saxon ship burial)
Woodbridge, Suffolk, IP12 3DJ

Weald and Downland Living Museum
(site of replica Anglo-Saxon hall)
Singleton, West Sussex, PO18 0EU

West Stow
(replica Anglo-Saxon village)
West Stow, Suffolk, IP28 6HG

Index